RATS!

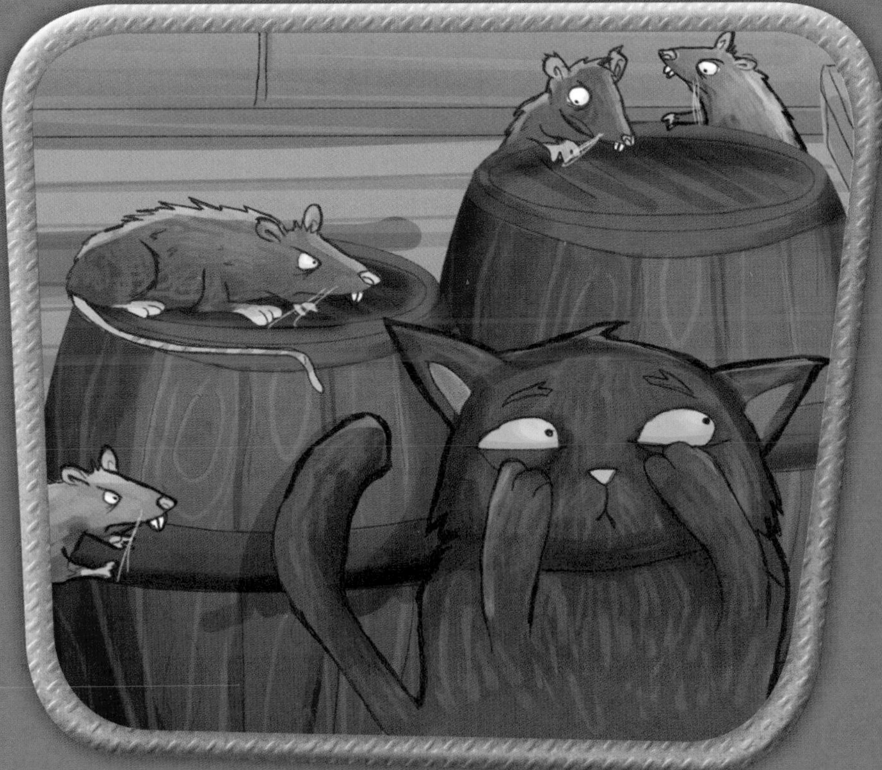

Written by Monica Hughes
Illustrated by Michael Emmerson

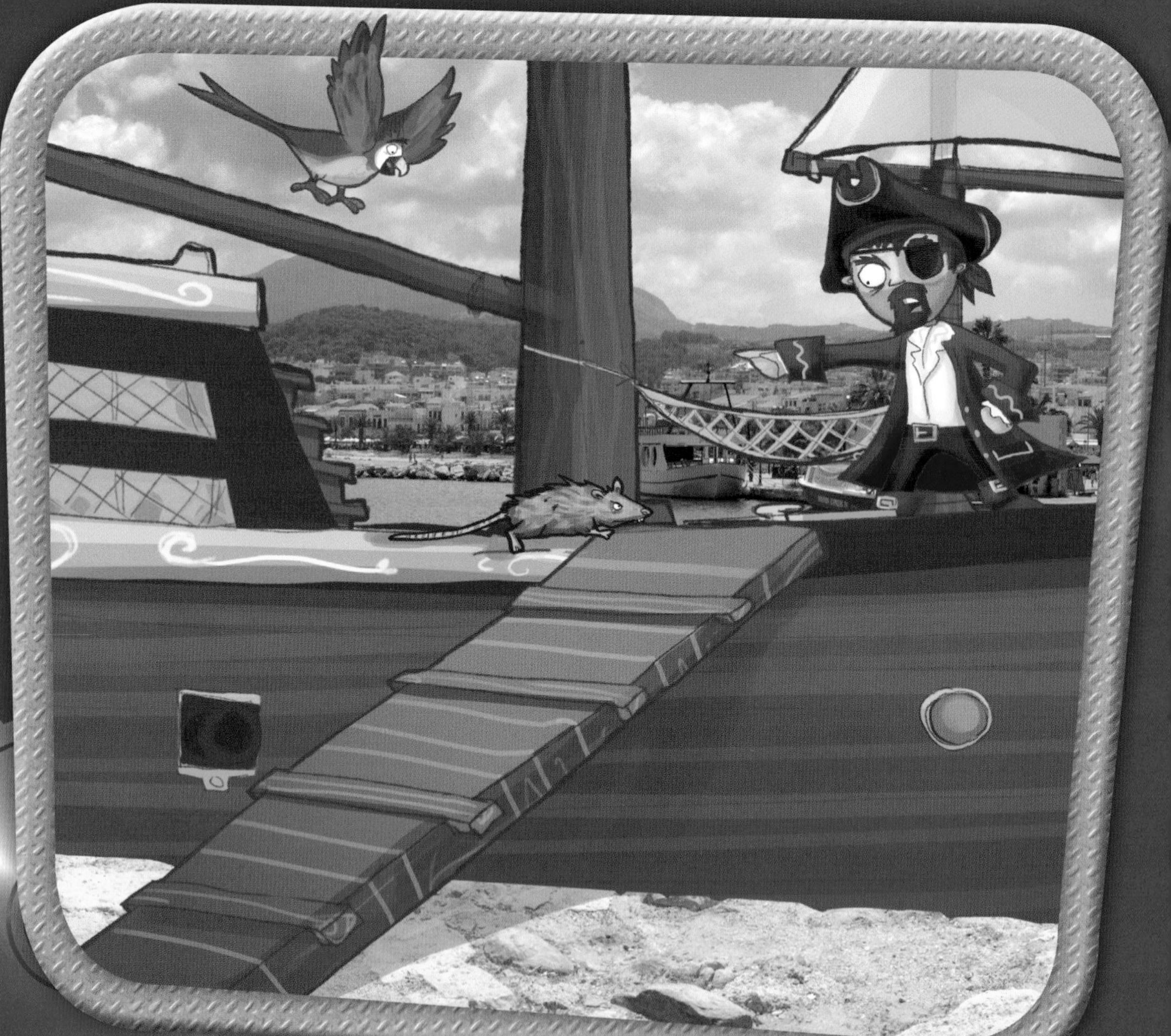

A rat! Pat is mad.

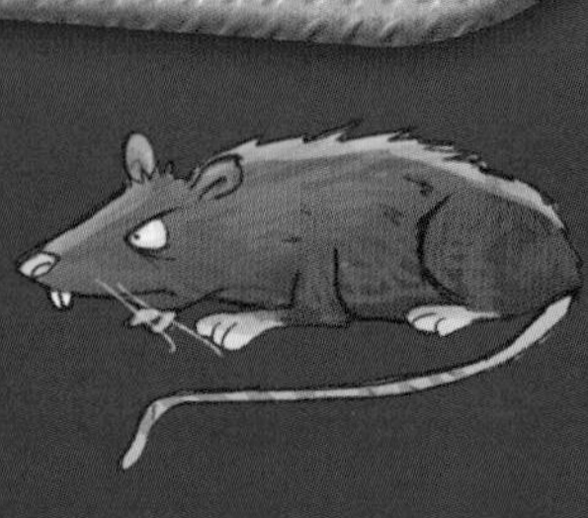

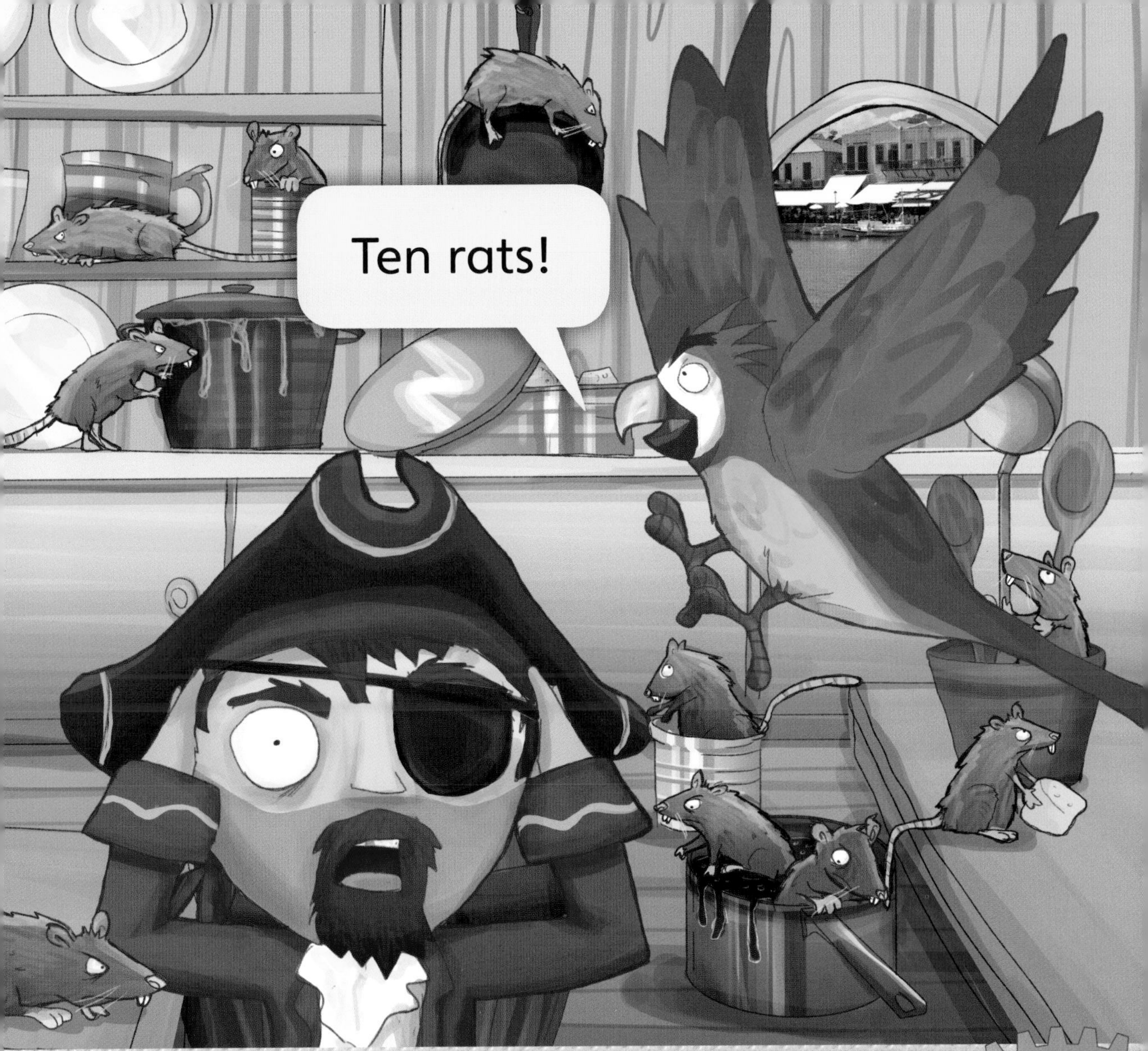

Rats in pans and tins.

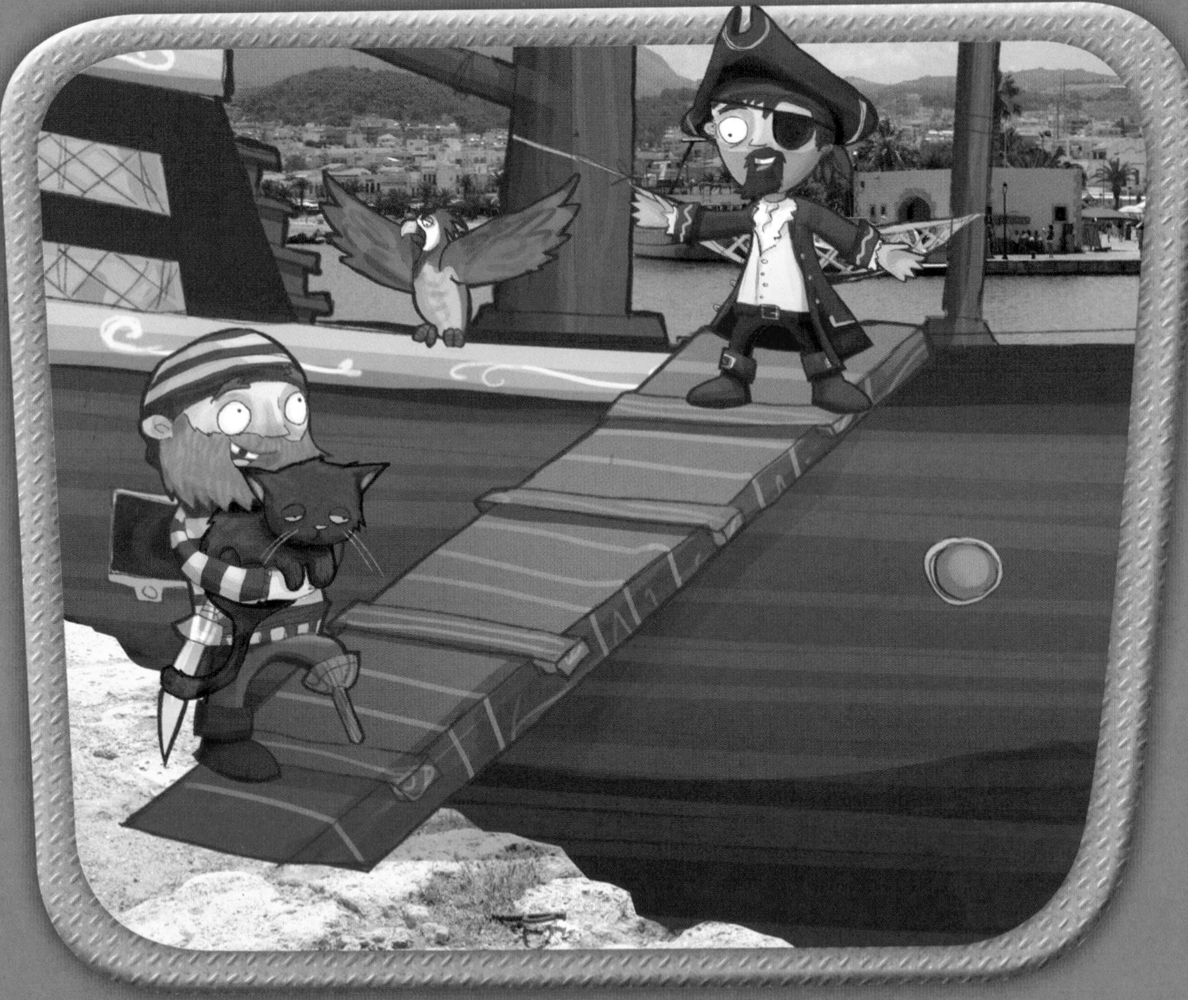

Red Ted had a cat.

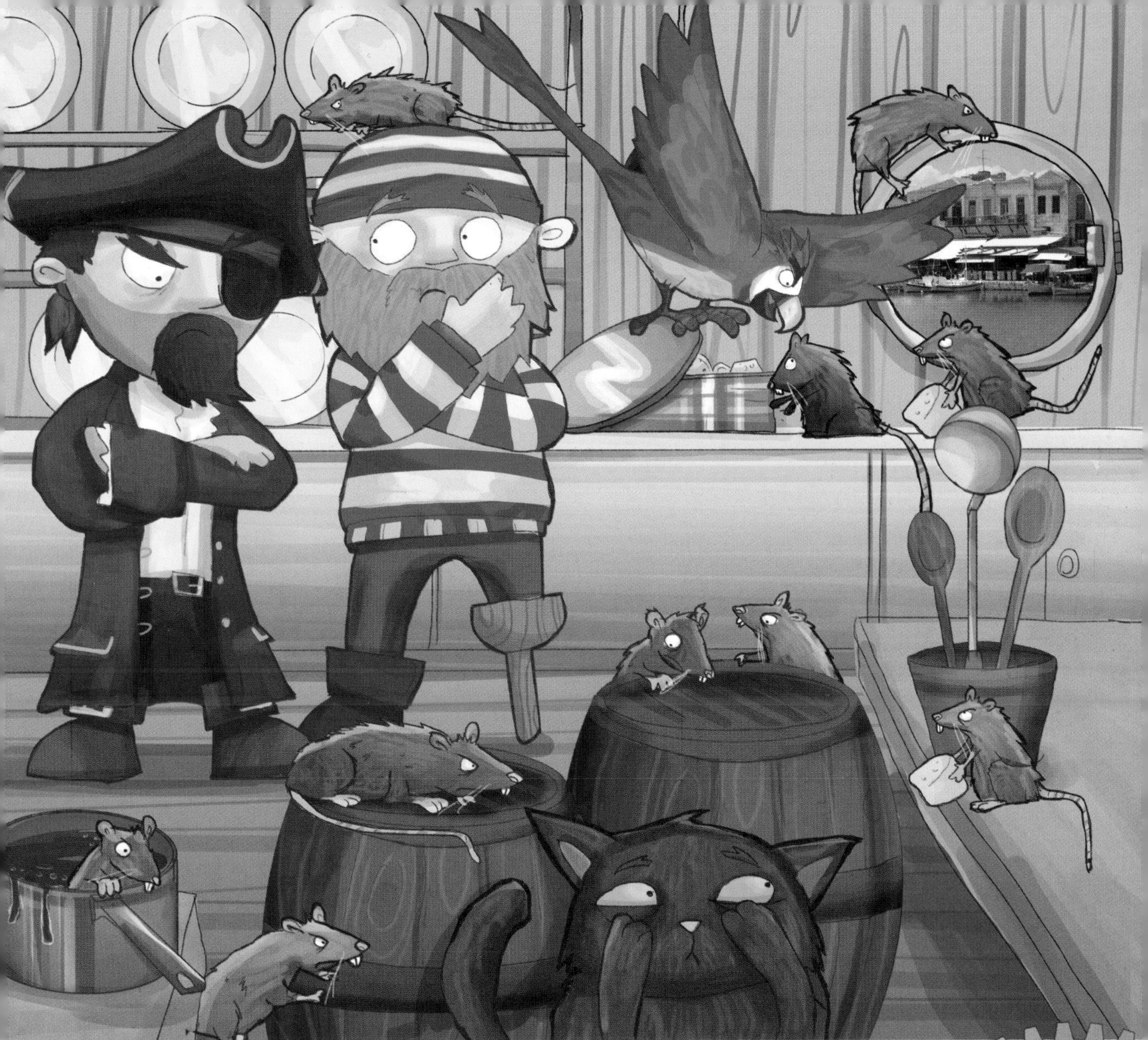

The cat hid.

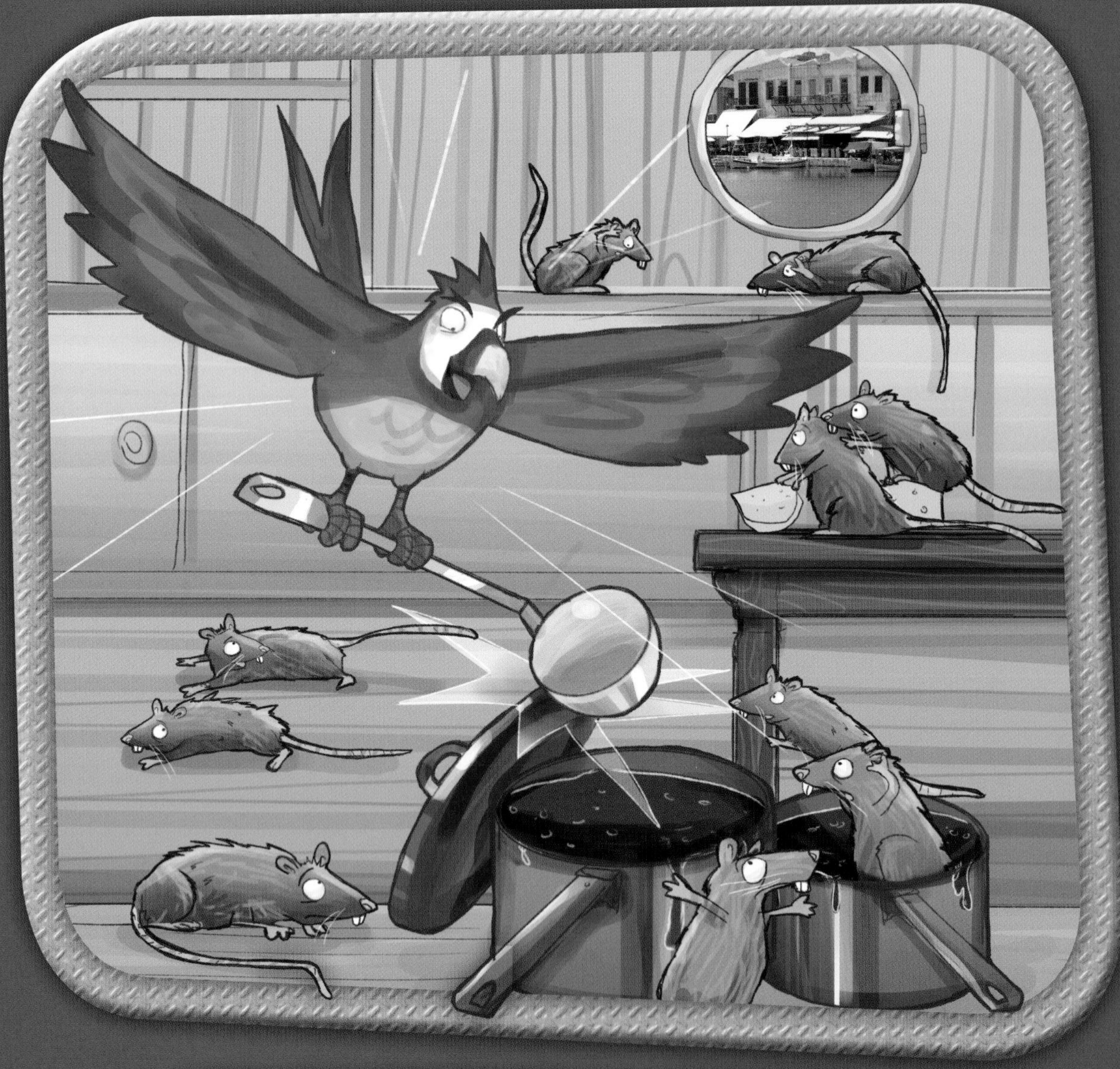

Sis hit the pans and tins.

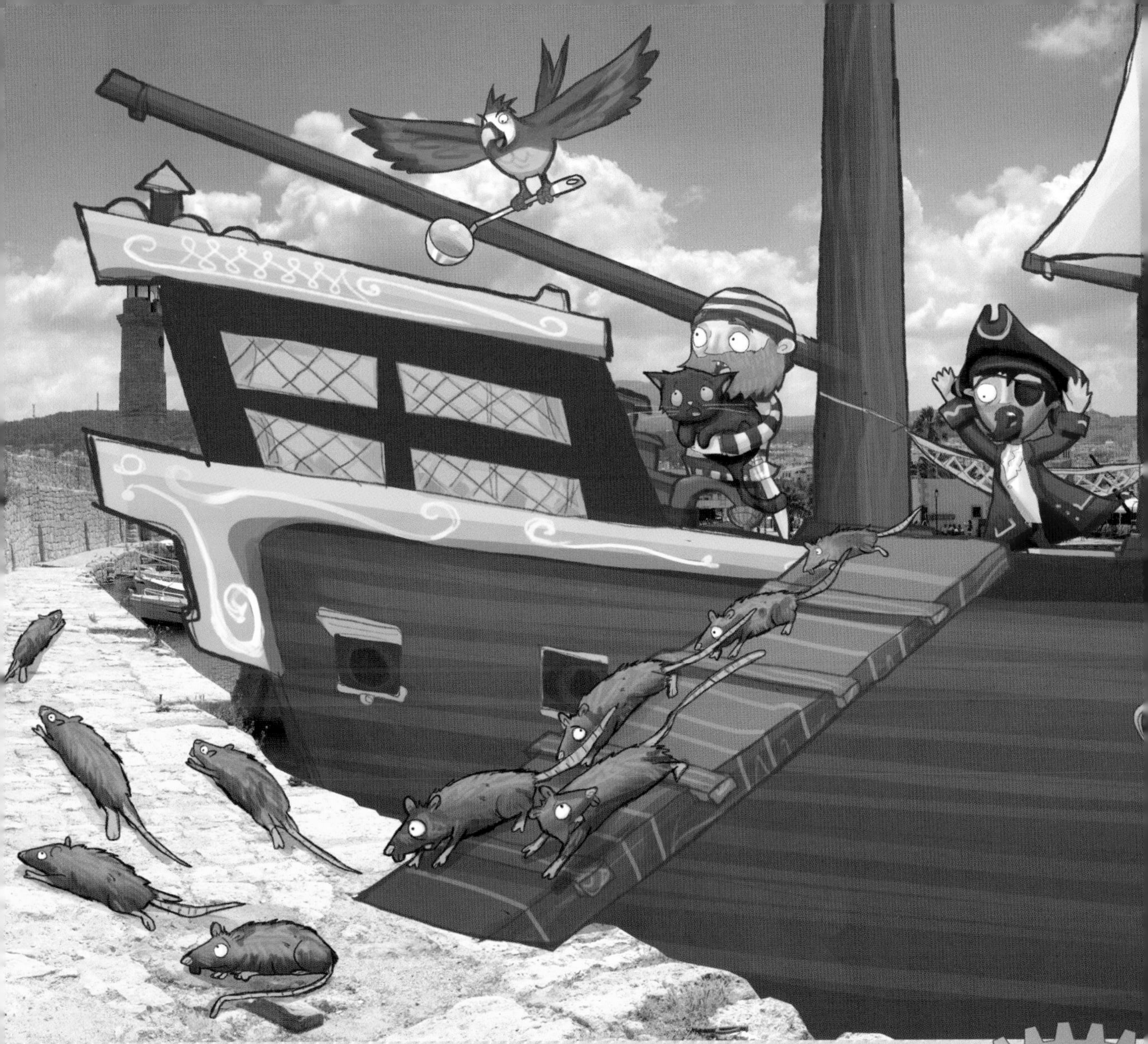

The rats ran.

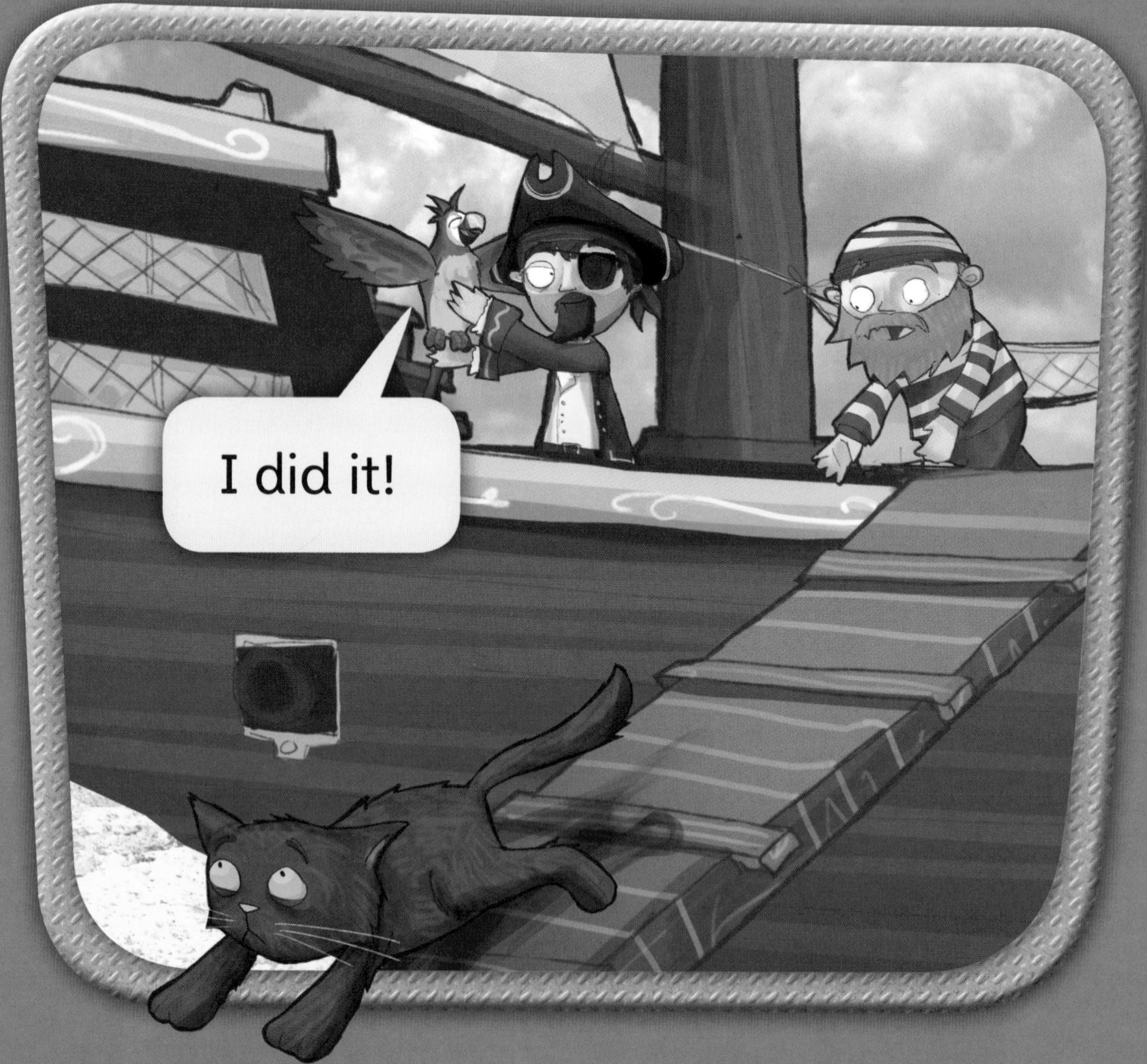

The cat ran.